The Owl and the Pussycat
AND OTHER NONSENSE

Edward Lear

The Owl and the Pussycat

AND OTHER NONSENSE

ILLUSTRATED BY

Robert Ingpen

templar publishing

This illustrated edition celebrating Edward Lear's bicentenary is dedicated to
a friend, the Honourable Tony Street, who is the great-great-grandson of
Edward Lear's sister, Sarah, and who was also it seems a talented artist and writer.

Robert Ingpen

A TEMPLAR BOOK

This edition published in 2012 by Templar Publishing,
an imprint of The Templar Company Limited,
The Granary, North Street, Dorking, Surrey, RH4 1DN, UK
www.templarco.co.uk

Originally created and produced by
PALAZZO EDITIONS LIMITED
2 Wood Street
Bath, BA1 2JQ
www.palazzoeditions.com

Illustrations © 2012 Robert Ingpen
Design and layout © 2012 Palazzo Editions Limited
Jacket cover design © 2012 by The Templar Company Limited

Art Director: Bernard Higton

1 3 5 7 9 10 8 6 4 2

ISBN 978-1-84877-346-2

A CIP catalogue record for this book is available from the British Library.

Printed and bound in China by Imago.

Contents

The Extraordinary Edward Lear

EDWARD LEAR was born in 1812, the twentieth child of a London stockbroker. When Lear was four his father's business collapsed and the family was pitched into poverty. As a young child he developed epilepsy, a condition regarded with much superstition in those days, and as a result, he always saw himself as somewhat of an outsider.

Neglected by his mother, Lear was primarily raised by his devoted sister, Ann, who did much to compensate for the unhappiness of his early years. She taught him to read and write, to play the piano and, most significantly, to draw and paint. As a young man he began to earn his living as an artist, first selling small drawings and later working as a draughtsman for the Zoological Society of London.

In 1832 Lear was engaged by Lord Stanley, the president of the Zoological Society, to make drawings of the rare birds and animals in the menagerie at his home, Knowsley Hall. Lear lived on the Knowsley estate for five years, and many of his beautiful drawings from this period are still in the library there. He would entertain Lord Stanley's children with his drawings and with limericks and nonsense rhymes that he made up for them – he noted that they responded with 'uproarious delight and welcome at the appearance of every new absurdity.'

By the mid 1830s, Lear decided to become a landscape painter and departed for Rome. He spent much of the rest of his life travelling throughout Europe, painting and writing a number of travel guides. His reputation as a painter grew and his works began to sell for considerable sums. In 1846 he was appointed drawing master to Queen Victoria, who had admired his illustrations in one of his travel books. But it was his nonsense verse – and the publication in 1870 of his most famous poem, *The Owl and the Pussycat* – that made him a household name. 'Nonsense is the breath of my nostrils,' he wrote. He saw it as a perfect medium to comment on the world around him – or, as he put it, 'this ludicrously whirligig life which one suffers from first and laughs at afterwards.'

Not long before Lear died in 1888, his friend Emily Tennyson wrote to him, 'However solitary your life has, for many years been, you must not forget that to you is given the most precious gift of peopling the lives of many, not only of this generation but of generations to come, with good and beautiful things and thoughts.'

Illustrator's Note

What is nonsense? As an introduction for the ninth edition of Edward Lear's *Nonsense Songs and Stories*, Sir Edward Strachey declared that 'Nonsense has shown itself to be a true work of the imagination, a child of genius, and its writing one of the fine arts... Nonsense has found the highest expression of itself in music, painting, sculpture and every form of poetry and prose... But as far as I know, Edward Lear first openly gave Nonsense its due place and honour when he called what he wrote pure and absolute Nonsense.'

Lear began a tradition that influenced many writers and performers in his lifetime and beyond, including Gilbert and Sullivan, A. A. Milne, Spike Milligan and The Goons, Dr. Seuss and Monty Python. To celebrate Lear and his contribution to our literature, I have revealed some botanical 'nonsense' that underlies his concept of a Bong-tree – a notion that recurs in many of his *Nonsense Songs and Stories*.

After he published his *Book of Nonsense* and just before one of his journeys from England to search abroad for what he titled 'the picturesque', Edward Lear wrote this letter to his close friend, Chichester Fortescue (see overleaf). It neatly sets out his biography written as if he thought he might not return.

Robert Ingpen

A Letter from Edward Lear

MY DEAR F.,

Born in 1812 (12th May), I began to draw, for bread and cheese, about 1827, but only did uncommon queer shop-sketches, selling them for prices varying from ninepence to four shillings: colouring prints, screens, fans; awhile making morbid disease drawings, for hospitals and certain doctors of physic. In 1831, through Mrs. Wentworth, I became employed at the Zoological Society, and in 1832, published "The Family of the Psittacidae," the first complete volume of coloured drawings of birds on so large a scale published in England, as far as I know unless Audubon's were previously engraved. J. Gould's "Indian Pheasants" were commenced at the same time, and after a little while he employed me to draw many of his birds of Europe, while I assisted Mrs. Gould in all her drawings of foregrounds, as may be seen in a moment by anyone who will glance at my drawings in G.'s European birds and the Toucans. From 1832 to 1836 when my health failed a good deal, I drew much at the Earl of Derby's; and a series of my drawings was published by Dr. Gray of the British Museum – a book now rare. In 1835 or '36, being in Ireland and the Lakes, I leaned more and more to landscape, and when in 1837 it was found that my health was more affected by the climate month by month, I went abroad, wintering in Rome till 1841, when I came to England and published a volume of lithographs called "Rome and its Environs." Returning to Rome, I visited Sicily and much of the South of Italy, and continued to make chalk drawings, though in 1840 I had painted my two first oil-paintings. I also gave lessons in drawing at Rome, and was able to make a very comfortable living. In 1845 I came again to England, and in 1846 gave Queen Victoria some lessons, through Her Majesty's having seen a work I published in that year on the Abruzzi, and another on the Roman States. In 1847 I went through all Southern Calabria, and again went round Sicily, and in 1848 left Rome entirely. I travelled then to Malta, Greece, Constantinople, and the Ionian Islands; and to Mount Sinai and Greece a second time in 1849, returning to England in that year. All 1850 I gave up to improving myself in figure-drawing, and I continued to paint oil-paintings till 1853, having published in the meantime, in 1849 and 1852, two volumes entitled "Journals of a Landscape Painter," in Albania and Calabria. The first edition of the "Book of Nonsense" was published in 1846, lithographed by tracing-paper. In 1854 I went to Egypt and Switzerland, and in 1855 to Corfu, where I remained the winters of 1856–57–58, visiting Athos, and, later, Jerusalem and Syria. In the autumn of 1858 I returned to England, and '59 and '60 winters were passed in Rome. 1861, I remained all the winter in England, and painted the Cedars of Lebanon and Masada, going after my sister's death in March, 1861, to Italy. The two following winters – '62 and '63 – were passed at Corfu, and at the end of the latter year I published "Views of the Ionian Islands." In 1862 a second edition of the "Book of Nonsense," much enlarged, was published, and is now in its sixteenth thousand.

O bother!

Yours affectionately, EDWARD LEAR.

EDWARD LEAR'S BIRDS FROM HIS EARLY DAYS AS A ZOOLOGICAL DRAUGHTSMAN, IN WHICH HE MANAGED TO CAPTURE NOT ONLY THE CHARACTERISTICS OF THE SPECIES BUT ALSO EACH BIRD'S INDIVIDUAL CHARACTER.

The Owl and the Pussycat

I

The Owl and the Pussycat went to sea
  In a beautiful pea-green boat,
    They took some honey, and plenty of money,
      Wrapped up in a five-pound note.
The Owl looked up to the stars above,
    And sang to a small guitar,
"O lovely Pussy! O Pussy, my love,
    What a beautiful Pussy you are,
          You are,
          You are!
What a beautiful Pussy you are!"

II

Pussy said to the Owl, "You elegant fowl!
　　How charmingly sweet you sing!
O let us be married; too long we have tarried:
　　But what shall we do for a ring?"
They sailed away for a year and a day,
　　To the land where the Bong-tree grows,
And there in a wood a Piggy-wig stood,
　　With a ring at the end of his nose,
　　　　　His nose,
　　　　　His nose,
With a ring at the end of his nose.

⟡ III ⟡

"Dear Pig, are you willing to sell for one shilling
    Your ring?" Said the Piggy, "I will."
So they took it away, and were married next day
    By the Turkey who lives on the hill.
They dined on mince, and slices of quince,
    Which they ate with a runcible spoon;
And hand in hand, on the edge of the sand,
    They danced by the light of the moon,
        The moon,
        The moon,
They danced by the light of the moon.

A Bong-tree Botany

VOL. II

CONSISTING OF
Elegantly Coloured Plates with Appropriate
Scientific and General Descriptions

of the Most Curious, Scarce and Beautiful

PRODUCTIONS OF NATURE

THAT HAVE RECENTLY BEEN DISCOVERED IN VARIOUS PARTS OF THE WORLD
AND DELINEATED BY THE ILLUSTRATOR ROBERT INGPEN.

PLATE ONE: THE BONG-TREE

Number One: THE BONG-FRUITING BUDS
Number Two: MATURE BONG-FRUIT *(As eaten by local insects and moths)*   *Number Three:* Unidentified
Number Four: IMMATURE BONG-FRUIT *(As eaten by the Common Bong Bird)*

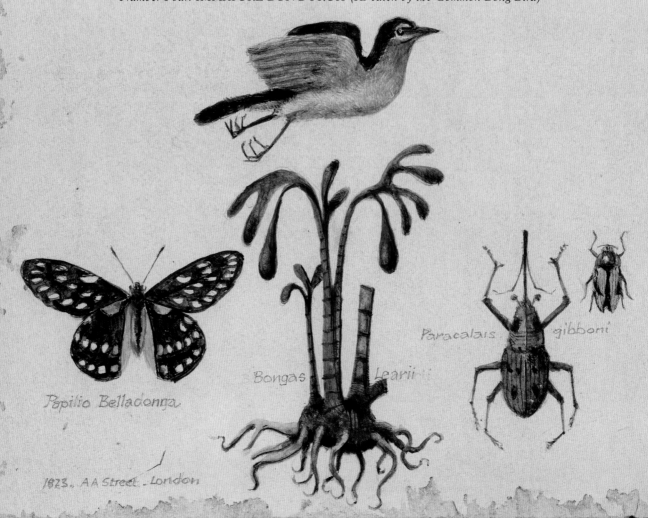

Papilio Belladonna

Bongas Learii

Paracalais gibboni

1823. A A Street. London

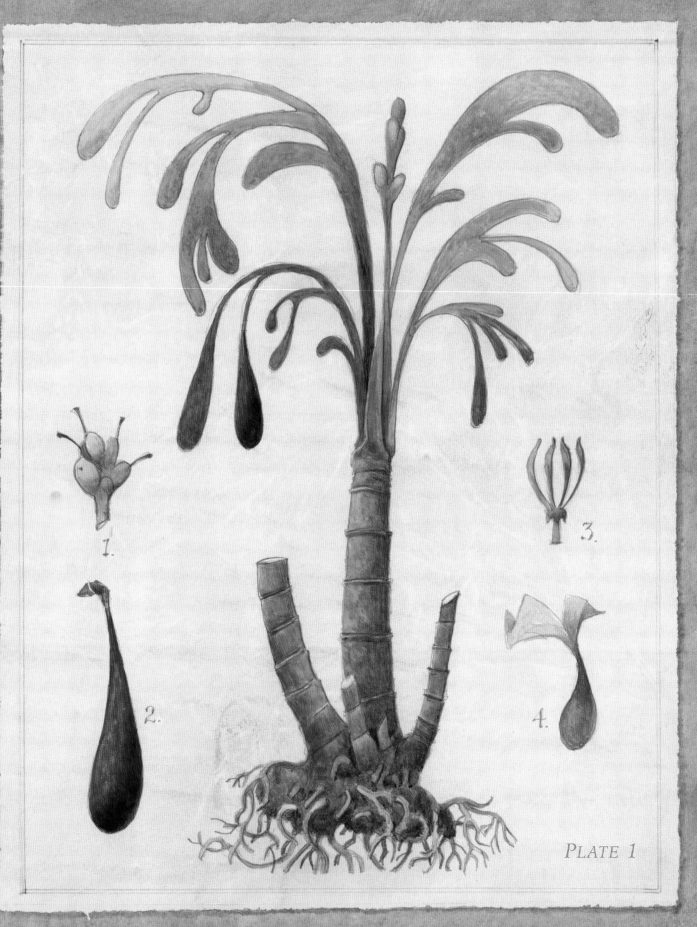

1.

2.

3.

4.

PLATE 1

Bong-tree Land

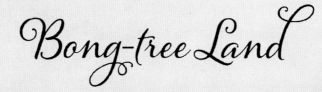

Visitors to Bong-tree Land must be prepared to travel by sea for a year and a day from almost any port in England. The Land, which is really an island, is almost completely covered with forests of self-sown Bong-trees (*Bongbusodae mangifera*). Botanists describe these rare plants as being related to bamboo grass that has the ability to produce fruit that ripen annually, then fall and rot if left alone. Bong-fruit is not unlike the common mango in taste, and can be used to make a delicate chutney that is usually eaten with mince (see recipe on page 48).

The Land boasts a few unexpected species of fauna and insects. Among these is a turkey who lives on the higher forest reaches, and who is uniquely qualified to perform marriages. The lower forest canopy is inhabited by pigs, some with rings in their noses, and all manner of insects that eat decaying Bong-fruit since humans rarely visit the Land to gather the annual crop.

For those intrepid tourists who do visit Bong-tree Land, the cuisine consists mainly of quince and mince combinations, which are traditionally eaten with a runcible spoon. Pig nose-rings can be bought for five new pence as souvenirs.

The Jumblies

I

They went to sea in a Sieve, they did,
  In a Sieve they went to sea:
In spite of all their friends could say,
On a winter's morn, on a stormy day,
  In a Sieve they went to sea!
And when the Sieve turned round and round,
And everyone cried, "You'll all be drowned!"
They called aloud, "Our Sieve ain't big,
But we don't care a button, we don't care a fig:
  In a Sieve we'll go to sea!"
    Far and few, far and few,
      Are the lands where the Jumblies live;
    Their heads are green, and their hands are blue,
      And they went to sea in a Sieve.

II

They sailed away in a Sieve, they did,
  In a Sieve they sailed so fast,
With only a beautiful pea-green veil
Tied with a ribbon, by way of a sail,
  To a small tobacco-pipe mast;
And everyone said, who saw them go,
"O won't they be soon upset, you know!
For the sky is dark, and the voyage is long,
And happen what may, it's extremely wrong
  In a Sieve to sail so fast!"
    Far and few, far and few,
      Are the lands where the Jumblies live;
    Their heads are green, and their hands are blue,
      And they went to sea in a Sieve.

⧼ III ⧽

The water it soon came in, it did,
   The water it soon came in;
So to keep them dry, they wrapped their feet
In a pinky paper all folded neat,
   And they fastened it down with a pin.
And they passed the night in a crockery-jar,
And each of them said, "How wise we are!
Though the sky be dark, and the voyage be long,
Yet we never can think we were rash or wrong,
   While round in our Sieve we spin!"
    Far and few, far and few,
      Are the lands where the Jumblies live;
      Their heads are green, and their hands are blue,
      And they went to sea in a Sieve.

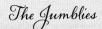

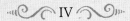

IV

And all night long they sailed away;
  And when the sun went down,
They whistled and warbled a moony song
To the echoing sound of a coppery gong,
  In the shade of the mountains brown.
"O Timballo! How happy we are,
When we live in a Sieve and a crockery-jar;
And all night long in the moonlight pale,
We sail away with a pea-green sail,
  In the shade of the mountains brown!"
    Far and few, far and few,
      Are the lands where the Jumblies live;
      Their heads are green, and their hands are blue,
      And they went to sea in a Sieve.

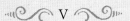

V

They sailed to the Western sea, they did,
  To a land all covered with trees,
And they bought an Owl, and a useful Cart,
And a pound of Rice, and a Cranberry Tart,
  And a hive of silvery Bees.
And they bought a Pig, and some green Jackdaws,
And a lovely Monkey with lollipop paws,
And forty bottles of Ring-Bo-Ree,
  And no end of Stilton Cheese.
    Far and few, far and few,
      Are the lands where the Jumblies live;
      Their heads are green, and their hands are blue,
      And they went to sea in a Sieve.

VI

And in twenty years they all came back,
   In twenty years or more,
And everyone said, "How tall they've grown!
For they've been to the Lakes, and the Terrible Zone,
   And the hills of the Chankly Bore;"
And they drank their health, and gave them a feast
Of dumplings made of beautiful yeast;
And everyone said, "If we only live,
We too will go to sea in a Sieve,
   To the hills of the Chankly Bore!"
    Far and few, far and few,
      Are the lands where the Jumblies live;
     Their heads are green, and their hands are blue,
      And they went to sea in a Sieve.

The Dong with a Luminous Nose

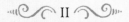

I

When awful darkness and silence reign
Over the great Gromboolian plain,
    Through the long, long wintry nights; –
When the angry breakers roar
As they beat on the rocky shore; –
    When Storm-clouds brood on the towering heights
Of the Hills of the Chankly Bore: –

II

Then, through the vast and gloomy dark,
There moves what seems a fiery spark,
    A lonely spark with silvery rays
    Piercing the coal-black night, –
    A meteor strange and bright: –
Hither and thither the vision strays,
    A single lurid light.

III

Slowly it wanders, – pauses, – creeps, –
Anon it sparkles, – flashes and leaps;
And ever as onward it gleaming goes
A light on the Bong-tree stems it throws.
And those who watch at that midnight hour
From Hall or Terrace, or lofty Tower,
Cry, as the wild light passes along, –
  "The Dong! – the Dong!
    The wandering Dong through the forest goes!
      The Dong! the Dong!
    The Dong with a luminous Nose!"

IV

    Long years ago
    The Dong was happy and gay,
Till he fell in love with a Jumbly Girl
    Who came to those shores one day.
For the Jumblies came in a Sieve, they did, –
Landing at eve near the Zemmery Fidd
    Where the Oblong Oysters grow,
    And the rocks are smooth and grey.
And all the woods and the valleys rang
With the Chorus they daily and nightly sang, –
    "Far and few, far and few,
      Are the lands where the Jumblies live;
    Their heads are green, and their hands are blue,
      And they went to sea in a Sieve."

V

Happily, happily passed those days!
　　　While the cheerful Jumblies staid;
　　They danced in circlets all night long,
　　To the plaintive pipe of the lively Dong,
　　　In moonlight, shine, or shade.
For day and night he was always there
By the side of the Jumbly Girl so fair,
With her sky-blue hands, and her sea-green hair;
Till the morning came of that hateful day
When the Jumblies sailed in their Sieve away,
And the Dong was left on the cruel shore
Gazing – gazing for evermore, –
Ever keeping his weary eyes on
That pea-green sail on the far horizon, –
Singing the Jumbly Chorus still
As he sat all day on the grassy hill, –
　　　"Far and few, far and few,
　　　　Are the lands where the Jumblies live;
　　　Their heads are green, and their hands are blue,
　　　　And they went to sea in a Sieve."

⟿ VI ⟾

But when the sun was low in the West,
 The Dong arose and said, –
 "What little sense I once possessed
Has quite gone out of my head!"
And since that day he wanders still
By lake and forest, marsh and hill,
Singing – "O somewhere, in valley or plain
Might I find my Jumbly Girl again!
For ever I'll seek by lake and shore
Till I find my Jumbly Girl once more!"

⟿ VII ⟾

 Playing a pipe with silvery squeaks,
 Since then his Jumbly Girl he seeks,
 And because by night he could not see,
 He gathered the bark of the Twangum Tree
  On the flowery plain that grows.
  And he wove him a wondrous Nose, –
 A Nose as strange as a Nose could be!
Of vast proportions and painted red,
And tied with cords to the back of his head.
 – In a hollow rounded space it ended
 With a luminous lamp within suspended,
  All fenced about
  With a bandage stout
  To prevent the wind from blowing it out; –
 And with holes all round to send the light,
 In gleaming rays on the dismal night.

VIII

And now each night, and all night long,
Over those plains still roams the Dong;
And above the wail of the Chimp and Snipe
You may hear the squeak of his plaintive pipe,
While ever he seeks, but seeks in vain,
To meet with his Jumbly Girl again;
Lonely and wild – all night he goes, –
The Dong with a luminous Nose!
And all who watch at the midnight hour,
From Hall or Terrace, or Lofty Tower,
Cry, as they trace the Meteor bright,
Moving along through the dreary night, –
　　"This is the hour when forth he goes,
　　The Dong with a luminous Nose!
　　Yonder – over the plain he goes;
　　　　He goes!
　　　　He goes;
　　The Dong with a luminous Nose!"

The New Vestments

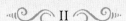

I

There lived an old man in the Kingdom of Tess,
Who invented a purely original dress;
And when it was perfectly made and complete,
He opened the door, and walked into the street.

II

By way of a Hat he'd a loaf of Brown Bread,
In the middle of which he inserted his head; –
His Shirt was made up of no end of dead Mice,
The warmth of whose skins was quite fluffy and nice; –
His Drawers were of Rabbit-skins; – so were his Shoes; –
His Stockings were skins, – but it is not known whose; –
His Waistcoat and Trousers were made of Pork Chops; –
His Buttons were Jujubes and Chocolate Drops; –
His Coat was all Pancakes, with Jam for a border,
And a girdle of Biscuits to keep it in order;
And he wore over all, as a screen from bad weather,
A Cloak of green Cabbage-leaves stitched all together.

III

He had walked a short way, when he heard a great noise,
Of all sorts of Beasticles, Birdlings, and Boys; –
And from every long street and dark lane in the town
Beasts, Birdles, and Boys in a tumult rushed down.
Two Cows and a Calf ate his Cabbage-leaf Cloak; –
Four Apes seized his Girdle, which vanished like smoke; –
Three Kids ate up half of his Pancaky Coat, –
And the tails were devoured by an ancient He Goat; –
An army of Dogs in a twinkling tore *up* his
Pork Waistcoat and Trousers to give to their Puppies; –

And while they were growling, and mumbling the Chops,
Ten Boys prigged the Jujubes and Chocolate Drops.
He tried to run back to his house, but in vain,
For scores of fat Pigs came again and again; –
They rushed out of stables and hovels and doors, –
They tore off his Stockings, his Shoes, and his Drawers; –
And now from the housetops with screechings descend,
Striped, spotted, white, black, and grey Cats without end,
They jumped on his shoulders and knocked off his Hat, –
When Crows, Ducks and Hens made a mincemeat of that; –
They speedily flew at his sleeves in a trice,
And utterly tore up his Shirt of dead Mice; –
They swallowed the last of his Shirt with a squall, –
Whereon he ran home with no clothes on at all.

And he said to himself as he bolted the door,
"I will not wear a similar dress any more,
Any more, any more, any more, never more!"

The Duck and the Kangaroo

I

Said the Duck to the Kangaroo,
 "Good gracious! how you hop
Over the fields and the water too,
 As if you never would stop!
My life is a bore in this nasty pond,
And I long to go out in the world beyond!
 I wish I could hop like you!"
 Said the Duck to the Kangaroo.

II

"Please give me a ride on your back!"
    Said the Duck to the Kangaroo.
"I would sit quite still, and say nothing but 'Quack,'
    The whole of the long day through!
And we'd go to the Dee, and the Jelly Bo Lee,
Over the land, and over the sea; –
    Please take me a ride! O do!"
    Said the Duck to the Kangaroo.

III

Said the Kangaroo to the Duck,
    "This requires some little reflection;
Perhaps on the whole it might bring me luck,
    And there seems but one objection,
Which is, if you'll let me speak so bold,
Your feet are unpleasantly wet and cold,
    And would probably give me the roo-
    Matiz!" said the Kangaroo.

IV

Said the Duck, "As I sat on the rocks,
    I have thought over that completely,
And I bought four pairs of worsted socks
    Which fit my web-feet neatly
And to keep out the cold I've bought a cloak,
And every day a cigar I'll smoke,
    All to follow my own dear true
    Love of a Kangaroo!"

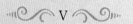

V

Said the Kangaroo, "I'm ready!
   All in the moonlight pale;
But to balance me well, dear Duck, sit steady!
   And quite at the end of my tail!"
So away they went with a hop and a bound,
And they hopped the whole world three times round;
   And who so happy, – O who,
   As the Duck and the Kangaroo?

Calico Pie

I

Calico Pie,
  The little birds fly
Down to the calico tree,
  Their wings were blue,
  And they sang "Tilly-loo!"
Till away they flew, –
And they never came back to me!
  They never came back!
  They never came back!
They never came back to me!

⠂⠒ II ⠒⠂

Calico Jam,
The little Fish swam
Over the syllabub sea,
He took off his hat,
To the Sole and the Sprat,
And the Willeby-wat, –
But he never came back to me!
He never came back!
He never came back!
He never came back to me!

⠂⠒ III ⠒⠂

Calico Ban,
The little Mice ran
To be ready in time for tea,
Flippity flup,
They drank it all up,
And danced in the cup, –
But they never came back to me!
They never came back!
They never came back!
They never came back to me!

IV

Calico Drum,
The Grasshoppers come,
The Butterfly, Beetle, and Bee
Over the ground,
Around and round,
With a hop and a bound, –
But they never came back!
They never came back!
They never came back!
They never came back to me!

How Pleasant to Know Mr. Lear!

"How pleasant to know Mr. Lear!"
    Who has written such volumes of stuff!
Some think him ill-tempered and queer,
    But a few think him pleasant enough.

His mind is concrete and fastidious,
    His nose is remarkably big;
His visage is more or less hideous,
    His beard it resembles a wig.

He has ears, and two eyes, and ten fingers,
    Leastways if you reckon two thumbs;
Long ago he was one of the singers,
    But now he is one of the dumbs.

He sits in a beautiful parlour,
    With hundreds of books on the wall;
He drinks a great deal of Marsala,
    But never gets tipsy at all.

He has many friends, laymen and clerical,
    Old Foss is the name of his cat;
His body is perfectly spherical,
    He weareth a runcible hat.

When he walks in waterproof white,
    The children run after him so!
Calling out, "He's gone out in his night-
    Gown, that crazy old Englishman, oh!"

He weeps by the side of the ocean,
    He weeps on the top of the hill;
He purchases pancakes and lotion,
    And chocolate shrimps from the mill.

He reads, but he cannot speak Spanish,
    He cannot abide ginger beer:
Ere the days of his pilgrimage vanish,
    How pleasant to know Mr. Lear!

A Recipe for Bong-fruit Chutney

1.35kg (3lbs) ripe Bong-fruit, peeled, halved and stoned*
75g (2½ oz) salt
2 litres (3½ pints) water
450g (1lb) sugar (in honey form)
600ml (1 pint) vinegar
75g (2½ oz) fresh quince powder, scraped
6 cloves of garlic, crushed
2 runcible spoons of medium hot chilli powder
1x50mm piece of cinnamon stick
125g (4½ oz) raisins
125g (4½ oz) dried dates, chopped
*Use green mangoes if Bong-fruit is unavailable

(Ask an adult to help you with this recipe.)

Drain the Bong-fruit pieces and set aside. Place the honey in a preserving pan and bring to the boil. Add remaining ingredients and bring back to the boil, stirring occasionally with the runcible spoon. Reduce the heat and simmer the chutney, stirring frequently until thick; then discard the cinnamon stick. Store in wooden barrels, ready to set sail.